SOUL FUEL

Daily Devotional To Ignite Your Faith

By

Dr. Veronia Lanie B. Decena-Magat

COPYRIGHT 2023@ SOUL FUEL
By Veronia `Lani B. Decena Magat

ISBN:
Hardbound-978-621-470-701-0
MOBI/KINDLE-978-621-470-702-7
Softbound/Paperback-978-621-470-703-4

Published by:
Poetry Planet Book Publishing House
Rosario, Pozorrubio, Pangasinan, Philippines
Contact Number: 09554960094
Email: maritesritumalta@gmail.com

DEDICATION

My husband and kid, who have been my rock throughout my life, are the inspiration for my book. Your unwavering love and encouragement have encouraged me to follow my dream of sharing the Gospel with the world.

I appreciate everyone who has supported me and believed in me throughout the years. To have your undying affection and support means the world to me.

This book is for everyone who, despite the world's distractions, is yearning to feel God's love and guidance. I pray that it helps you feel better, gives you faith, and motivates you to find your life's true calling.

This book is meant to be a constant reminder that God is there, even when it seems like the world is falling apart around us.

I appreciate you coming along on this adventure with me.

Thank God for you with affection and appreciation,

~Lani

TABLE OF COTENTS

PREFACE

It's easy to let stress, anxiety, and tiredness weigh us down in today's hectic world. It's vital to stop amid our busy lives to replenish our spirits.

This book, Soul Fuel, is an exploration of how God can refresh and reinvigorate us.

My week has been quite hectic. It's hard to keep track of the days between work and other commitments. But I do my best to squeeze in some quiet time for meditation and prayer even amid all this activity. For me, maintaining a relationship with God is crucial to overcoming the difficulties I face daily.

It has been a struggle, not always simple, to find grace in all that I do. But by developing an attitude of appreciation and praying for God's insight and direction, I have learned to face difficulties in life with self-assurance and composure.

I felt a strong motivation to write this book, a summons from God to spread His love. My prayer is that this little book would encourage and raise its readers, moving them closer to God and into His loving embrace. Soul Fuel provides a daily dose of God's grace by reiterating the greatness of God's love and mercy via Scripture, words from the saints, and personal tales.

Monday

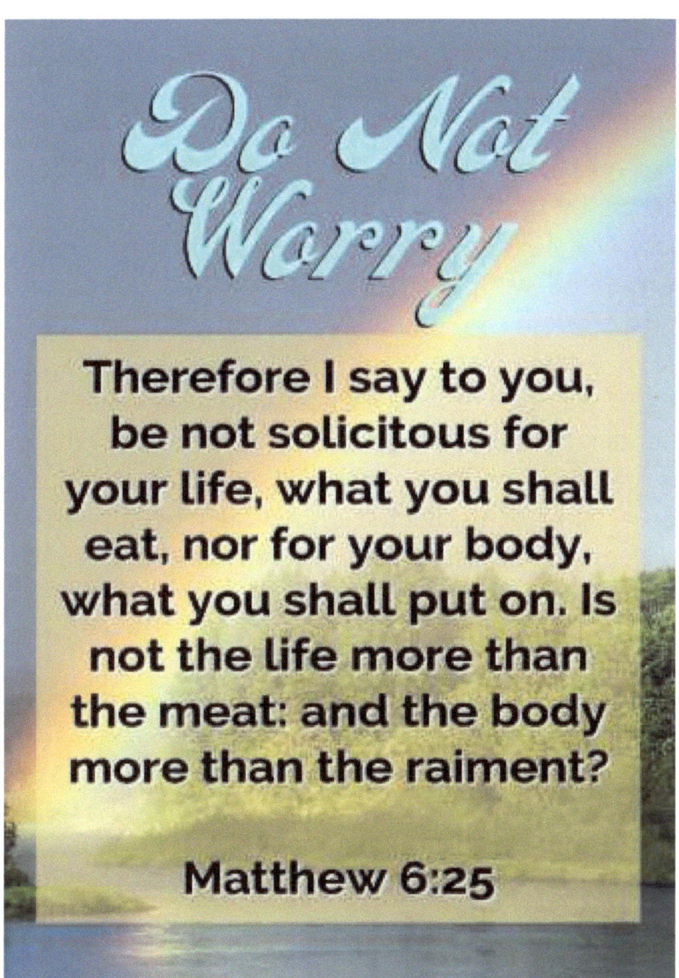

Do Not Worry

Therefore I say to you,
be not solicitous for
your life, what you shall
eat, nor for your body,
what you shall put on. Is
not the life more than
the meat: and the body
more than the raiment?

Matthew 6:25

One Jack lost his work and found it difficult to make ends meet. He needed to provide for his family and pay the rent. He was fretting over how he would feed his family one day as he sat on his veranda.

At that moment, Jack's next-door neighbor strolled by and noticed the look of concern on his face. The next-door neighbor assured them, "Don't worry, God will provide." Jack, who did not place much stock in religion, simply shrugged.

A buddy of Jack's called a few days later to offer him a job with a significantly greater salary than his previous position. Jack felt both startled and appreciative. He reflected on his neighbor's advice and concluded that he must have confidence and trust in God.

Tuesday

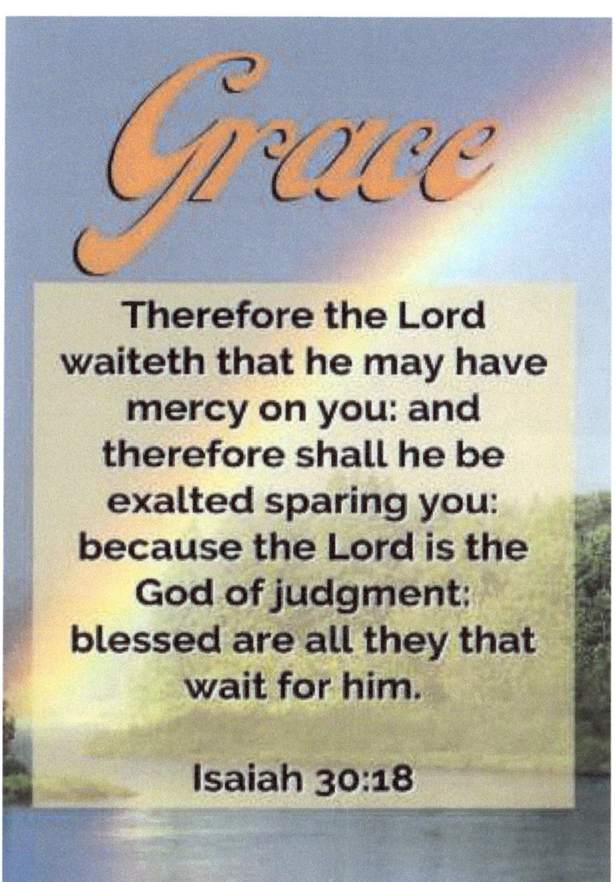

Grace
Therefore the Lord waiteth that he may have mercy on you: and therefore shall he be exalted sparing you: because the Lord is the God of judgment; blessed are all they that wait for him.

Isaiah 30:18

There was a man named Peter who resided in a rural community long ago. Peter was a dedicated farmer who worked long hours to provide for his family. A severe drought attacked the community one day, killing off Peter's crops.

Peter was heartbroken and worried about the future of his family. But he never stopped believing in God's providence and praying for it.

A bunch of strangers arrived in town one day and made Peter a substantial offer for his farm. Peter was reluctant at first, but he knew deep down that he had to do it since it was God's will.

Peter took the deal and used the funds to support his family and launch a new enterprise. Peter realized then that even in the darkest of circumstances, God's grace would see him through.

Wednesday

Hope
Blessed be the man that trusteth in the Lord, and the Lord shall be his confidence.
Jeremiah 17:7

Michelle sat in her cell, contemplating the unfairness she had experienced. She had been imprisoned for a total of two years after being wrongfully convicted of a crime she had not committed. But in the confines of her cell, she found comfort in God's presence via prayer. She beseeched the heavens for fortitude, bravery, and fairness. And then, after what felt like an age, a ray of light appeared. The charges against her were dropped, and she was let free. She praised God with happy tears streaming down her face.

Thursday

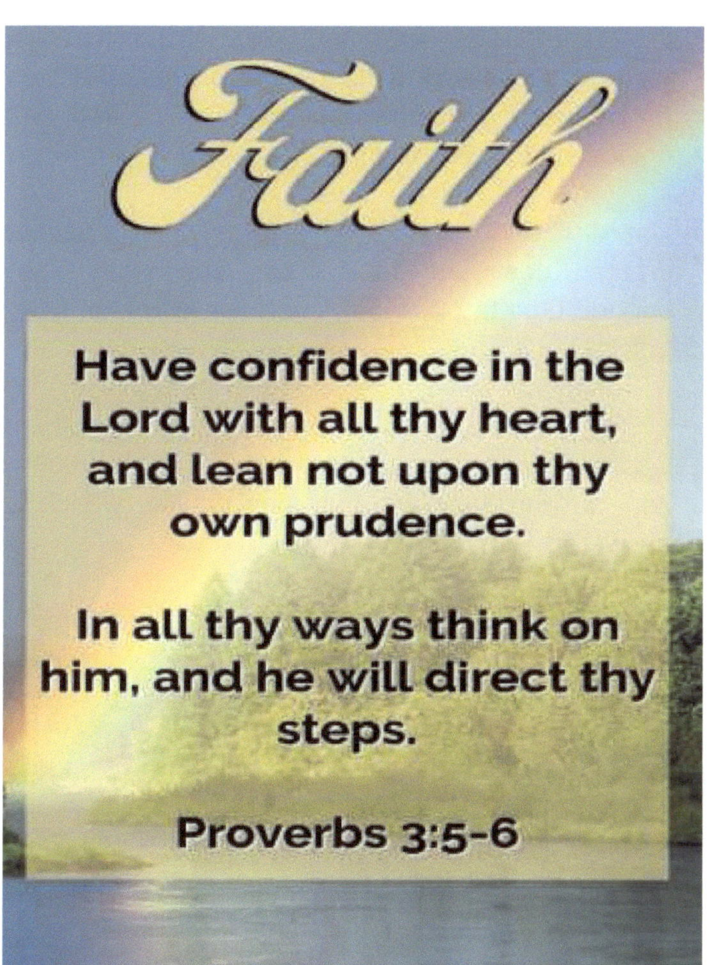
Faith
Have confidence in the Lord with all thy heart, and lean not upon thy own prudence.

In all thy ways think on him, and he will direct thy steps.

Proverbs 3:5-6

A hillside settlement once stood amongst verdant woods and rushing water. The people were revered for their unshakeable faith in God and their dedication to a life of simplicity.

The locals were devastated when a severe drought destroyed their crops one year. They begged God to pity them, and their faith kept them going.

Weeks slipped into months, and still, there was no respite in sight. The people of the community kept praying, believing that their prayers would be answered.

The village was caught off guard by a torrential downpour on a sunny day, but the resulting flood provided much-needed water. The people's confidence in God returned as their harvests flourished.

The peasants trusted that God would provide for them no matter how difficult conditions got. Their unwavering faith is what kept them going through the darkest circumstances.

Friday

Love

Charity is patient, is kind: charity envieth not, dealeth not perversely; is not puffed up;

Is not ambitious, seeketh not her own, is not provoked to anger, thinketh no evil;

Rejoiceth not in iniquity, but rejoiceth with the truth;

Beareth all things, believeth all things, hopeth all things, endureth all things.

Charity never falleth away: whether prophecies shall be made void, or tongues shall cease, or knowledge shall be destroyed.

1 Corinthians 13:4-8

There was a little girl who had trouble finding her place in the world. Nothing she encountered on her quest for love or direction satisfied her empty soul. She happened upon a church one day and decided to check it out. She sat in the church pews, eyes closed, and prayed. She felt God's love flood over her suddenly, and she knew it was good. After that, she knew that God's love would always provide for her, so she committed herself to a life of service to others. She lived a happy, blessed life, so it must have.

Saturday

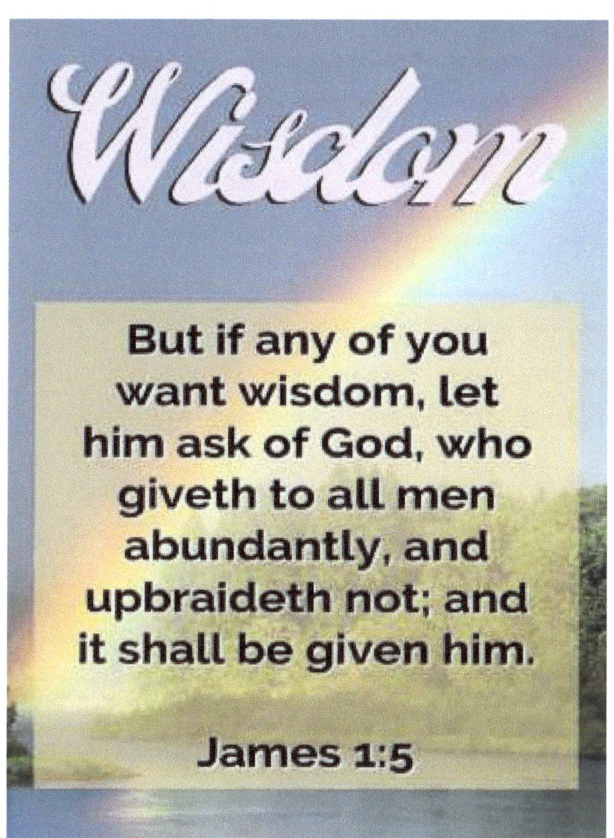
Wisdom
But if any of you
want wisdom, let
him ask of God, who
giveth to all men
abundantly, and
upbraideth not; and
it shall be given him.

James 1:5

Nathan was an example of wisdom. He was certain that there was a purpose behind every occurrence. His cancer diagnosis, though, caused him to reevaluate his faith. He couldn't fathom why God would let him endure such an agonizing condition.

As he received therapy, he came to terms with the fact that his illness was God's method of speaking to him. He realized he needed to take things more slowly and enjoy life more. He learned to appreciate the simple pleasures in life and spend more time with his loved ones.

Nathan's cancer experience gave him a fresh outlook on life. He realized the importance of the here and now and the will of God. He felt privileged to have obtained such insight and was resolved to share it with others. He finds wisdom in his suffering and unites his disease to the cross of our Lord Jesus.

Sunday

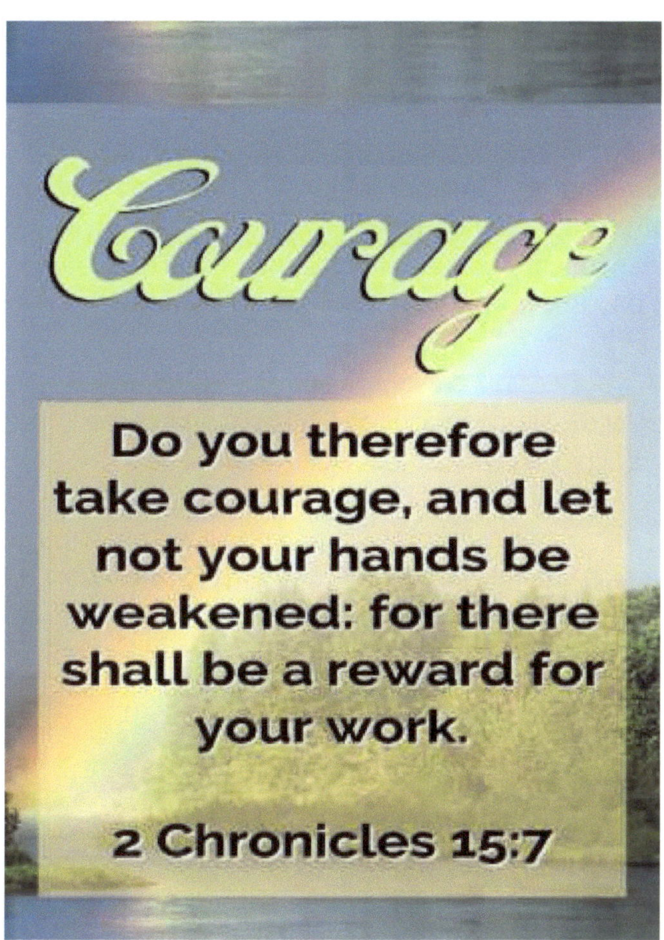

Courage

Do you therefore take courage, and let not your hands be weakened: for there shall be a reward for your work.

2 Chronicles 15:7

Sarah was a village girl. A nasty and dishonest monarch taxed her village heavily. The king chastised Sarah's father for not paying taxes one day.

Sarah warned the locals about the king's corruption to save her father. She revealed that her father had paid all taxes. Sarah's bravery gave the peasants the courage to face the king. They refused to pay taxes until the king's laws were revealed.

Sarah's bravery made the king realize his mistakes. He apologized to the locals and swore to rule justly from then on.

Sarah's honesty saved her father and brought harmony to the village. She was glad for the lesson of never compromising truth and that God had protected her and her family.

DAILY PRAYERS

Morning Prayer on Monday

Morning Prayer on Monday
God, please guide and strengthen me this week.
Help me follow your ways and serve you in
everything. Bless me and my family and friends.
Amen.

Morning Prayer on Tuesday

Thank you, Lord God. Life, health, and strength—
thank you. Help me be kind and caring throughout
the day. Give me the insight to make good
decisions and impact others. Amen.

Morning Prayer on Wednesday

Heavenly Father, please help me release my concerns, anxieties, and worries today. Love and peace me. Help me trust your life plan and promises. Help me with everything. Amen.

Morning Prayer on Thursday

I give you my pleasures, sorrows, and problems today, God.
May your grace help me overcome any challenges. Help me be patient, kind, and forgiving. Bless my loved ones.
Amen.

Morning Prayer on Friday

Father, please watch over me today. Grant me wisdom, knowledge, and understanding to complete my tasks. Help me be productive and benefit others. God bless you today. Amen.

Morning Prayer on Saturday

Lord, today I begin with humility and thanks. Help me remember others' needs and offer assistance when needed. I want your love and grace all day. Give me the courage to conquer obstacles. Amen.

Morning Prayer on Sunday

I dedicate this week to you, God. May your love radiate through me. Help me be kind, patient, and forgiving to everyone. Bless me and my family. Amen.

EVENING PRAYER

Evening Prayer on a Monday

At day's end, I come to you, Lord Jesus, to seek your pardon for any sins I may have committed today. Thank you for your compassion; please bless me with your restorative power. Please keep me safe and secure tonight so that I can sleep soundly. Amen.

Prayer on a Tuesday Night:

Please accept my gratitude, Lord, for this day and everything it has brought. If I have done anything wrong today, please forgive me. Please remove any sources of distress from my life, whether physical or mental, so that I may be restored and strengthened. This evening and throughout the night, please keep my loved ones and me safe. Amen.

Prayers for Wednesday Evening:

Jesus, I have a contrite spirit as I approach you now. Please pardon me for any wrongs I may have committed today. I appreciate everything you have done in my life and all the wonderful individuals you have placed in it. Please cure me of my ailments and shield me from harm. Please also look for my loved ones and me as we sleep tonight. Amen.

Evening Prayer on a Thursday:

Please forgive me, Lord, for any wrongdoings I may have done today. Your daily grace and mercy refresh me, and for that, I am eternally grateful. Please alleviate my suffering, both mental and physical, and keep me safe tonight. Please give me the fortitude and wisdom to serve you in the best way possible. Amen.

Prayers on a Friday Night:

Oh Lord, If I offended anyone here today, please accept my apologies. Thank you for keeping me safe this week and for all the benefits you have bestowed upon me. Please cure me of all my ailments so that I may be healthy and powerful. Tonight, I lay my hope in your kindness as I sleep. Amen.

Prayers on a Saturday Night:

I pray for forgiveness from the Lord for any wrongdoing I may have done today. I appreciate all the people who have shown their affection for me and me. Please mend my broken body and soothe my aching heart, and keep me safe from harm when night falls. I ask that you bless my family and friends and provide them with rest. Amen.

Prayers on Sunday Evening:

Please pardon me, Lord Jesus, for all my wrongdoings on this day of rest. I appreciate all the good things in my life and the people who have made them possible. Please relieve my suffering, both mental and physical, and shield me from harm. I pray for tranquility, love, and happiness as I embark on this new day. Amen.

Things To Ponder

(Smile, Be Happy, and Be Grateful! God Loves you!)

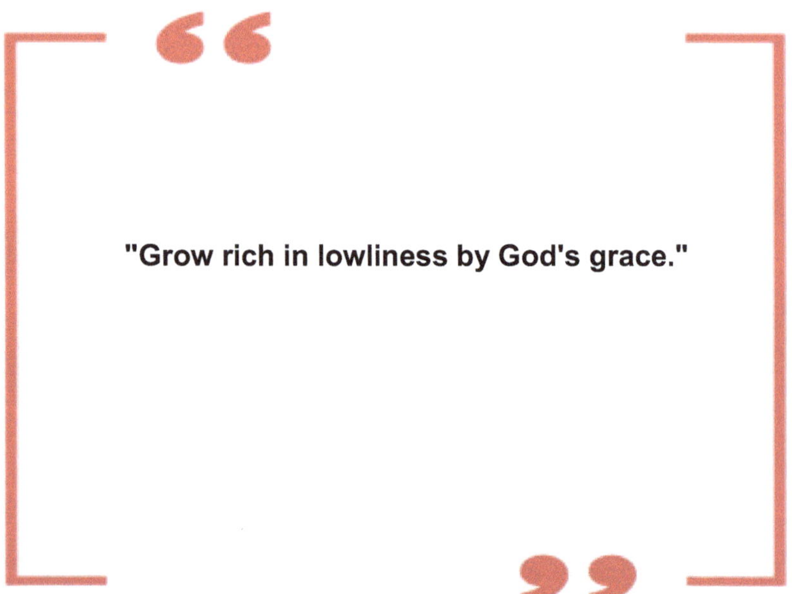
"Grow rich in lowliness by God's grace."

"Prayer is not a means to an end, but the end itself: a beautiful union with God that brings immense joy and peace in life."

~Doc Lani

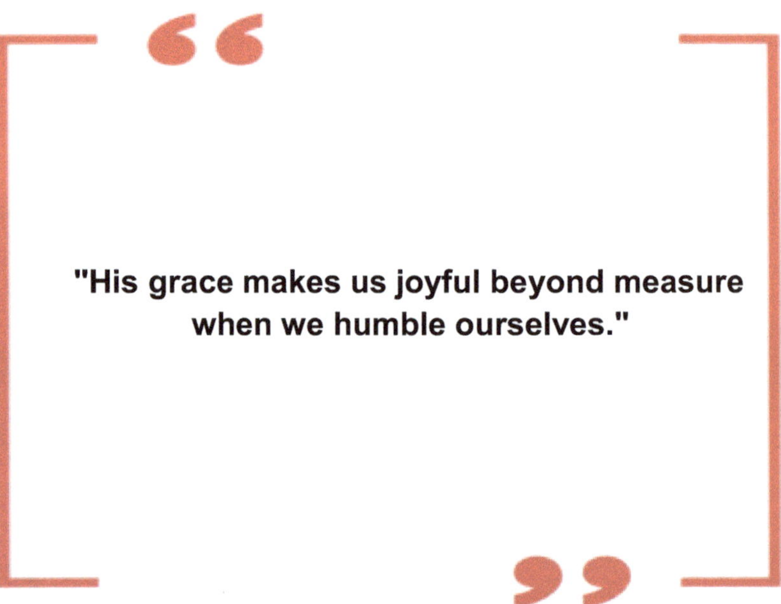
"His grace makes us joyful beyond measure
when we humble ourselves."

"Trusting God brings a sense of security that nothing else can offer. It allows us to let go, surrender and find true freedom in His will."

~Doc Lani

"God doesn't want to burden us, He wants to ease our pain, learn to detach from the world and attached to God"

"Asking forgiveness is not just an act of humility, but a doorway to true healing and restoration in life."
~Doc Lani

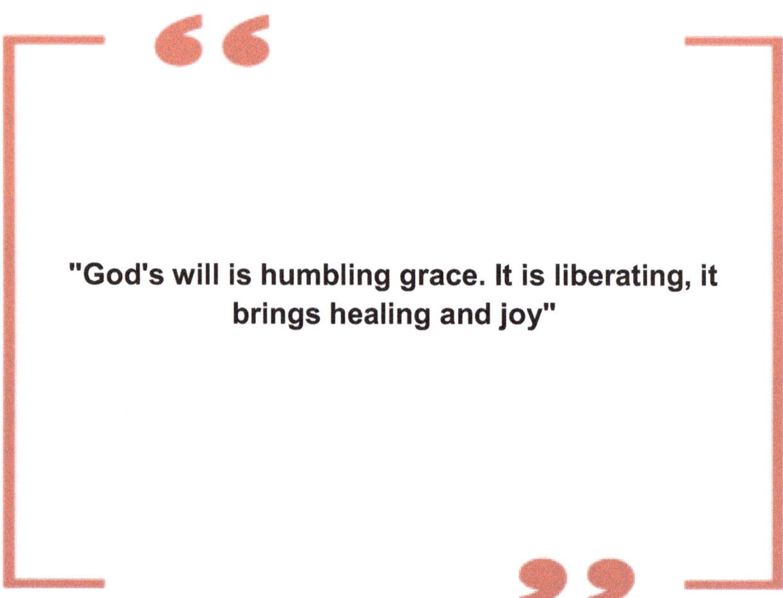
"God's will is humbling grace. It is liberating, it brings healing and joy"

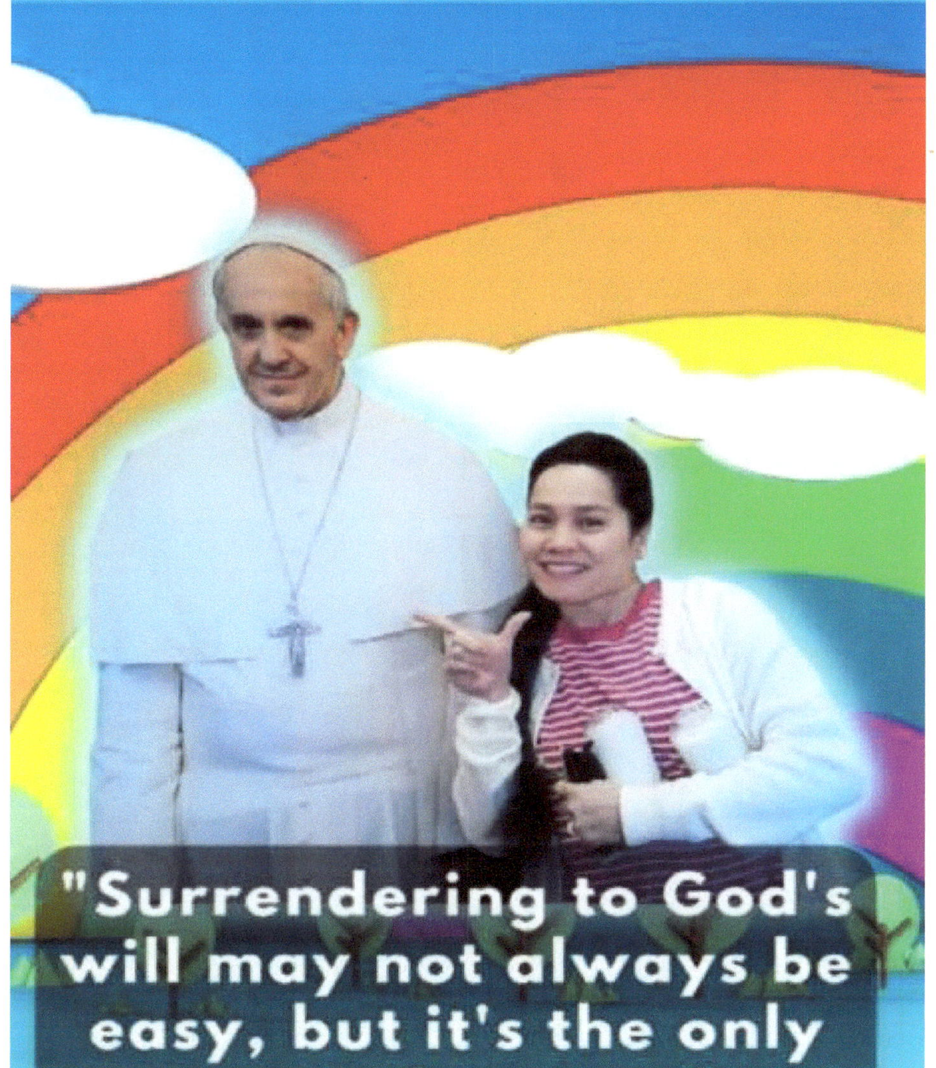

"Surrendering to God's will may not always be easy, but it's the only way to truly experience the fullness of joy and purpose in life."

~Doc Lani

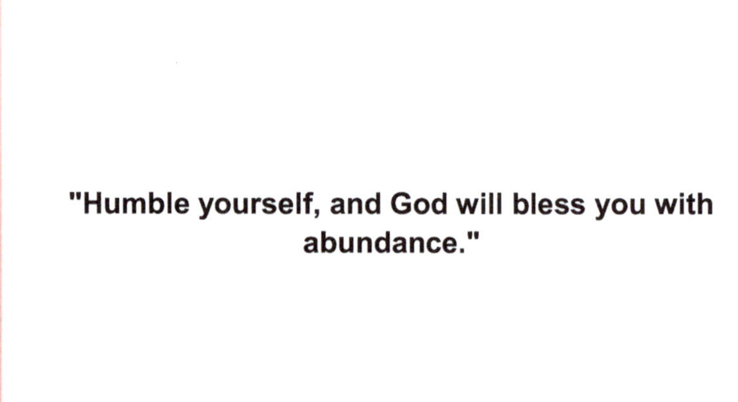

"Humble yourself, and God will bless you with abundance."

"Prayer is the anchor that keeps us grounded and connected with God, guiding us towards His divine plan for our lives."

~Doc Lani

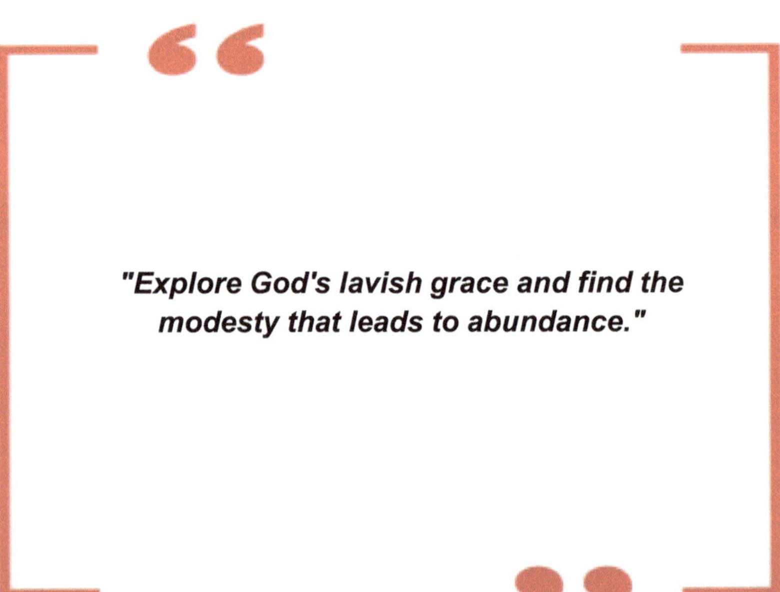

"Explore God's lavish grace and find the modesty that leads to abundance."

"Trusting God in the midst of uncertainty unlocks a peace that surpasses all understanding and brings joy that cannot be shaken."

~Doc Lani

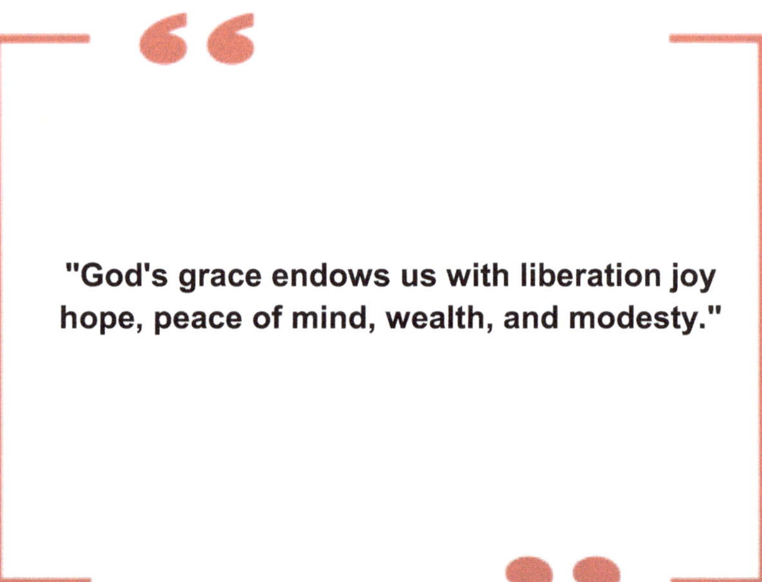

"God's grace endows us with liberation joy
hope, peace of mind, wealth, and modesty."

"As we surrender our plans to God and trust in His sovereignty, we find ourselves on a path that leads to life and joy beyond measure."

~Doc Lani